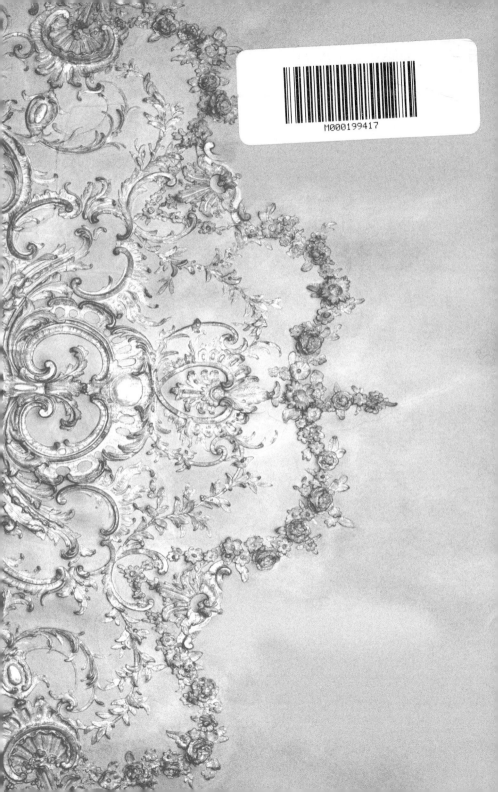

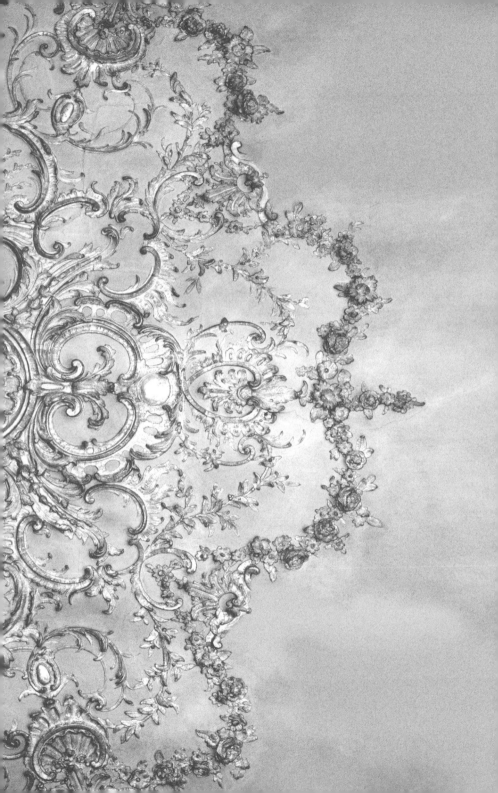

Design by Hana Anouk Nakamura
Calligraphy by Nim Ben-Reuven

ISBN 978-1-4197-2691-0

Photographs © 2017 Georgianna Lane

Printed and bound in China
10 9 8 7 6 5 4 3 2 1

Abrams Noterie products are available at special discounts when
purchased in quantity for premiums and promotions as well as
fundraising or educational use. Special editions can also be created to
specification. For details, contact specialsales@abramsbooks.com or
the address below.

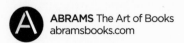

ABRAMS The Art of Books
abramsbooks.com